THE FOSSA

Do Your Kids Know This?

A Children's Picture Book
Amazing Creature Series

Tanya Turner

PUBLISHED BY:

Tanya Turner

Copyright © 2016

TABLE OF CONTENTS

The Fossa 6

Getting to Know the Fossa 7

Where Can You Find Fossas? 12

How Fossas Behave 13

Diet 17

How Do Fossas Communicate? 18

Breeding and Reproduction 20

Life Span of Fossa 22

Status 23

THE FOSSA

The Fossa

The Fossa.
Image from Shutterstock by belizar.

Just one look at the Fossa and you will see its similarity to a cat. It's not a cat – although it does have a lot of similarities to a cat, even in its behavior.

The Fossa has also been compared to the cougar, which is known as puma, mountain lion, and panther – and all those animals also look like a cat.

Like all other animals, however, the Fossa has its own unique characteristics. So, let's get to know this animal better, shall we?

Side view of a Fossa.
Image from Shutterstock by Alan Jeffery

Getting to Know the Fossa

The Fossa is the largest meat-eating mammal in Madagascar. An adult Fossa has a body length of 28 to 31 inches and they can weigh anywhere from 12 to 19 pounds. In this particular type of animal, the males are larger than the females. The males can be anywhere from 14 to 19 pounds, while the females will only weigh about 12 to 15 pounds.

Of course, there will always be smaller and bigger Fossas than the average size. In fact, there are reported cases of really large Fossas that weigh up to about 40 pounds.

Like cats, Fossas have claws too, and these are semi-retractable. Although they can make their claws longer and shorter, they can't totally hide them in their paws. Aside from using their claws to defend themselves from their enemies, Fossas also use them for climbing trees. Remember, this type of animal spends a lot of time in trees, so they need their claws to hold on tightly to the branches of trees. Without their claws, they can easily slip and fall when they're up there.

Fossas have muscular bodies – which showcase their strength. Their ankles are also very flexible to allow them to easily climb up and down trees. In fact, they can climb up and down trees with their head first, and they can also jump from tree to tree without any trouble at all. Their feet even have strong pads to support their weight. All these features are really important when they're hunting for prey. Prey is live food that Fossas hunt, and sometimes, they need to chase them among tree branches.

Fossas can climb trees.
Image from Shutterstock by David Thyberg.

It's important to note that Fossas have large heads – well, larger than a cat's head, since their whole bodies are bigger than cats, too. What's really amazing is that they have very long tails – these will be almost the same length as their bodies. For a 25-inch long Fossa, its tail will also be about 25 inches long. Note, too, that they also use their tail for balancing – especially when they are in trees.

Fossas have brown eyes that are set apart from each other. Their pupils can also constrict to a slit when it's not dilated. At night, however, their eyes will reflect the color of orange when hit by light.

Fossas can see, hear, and smell very well.
Image from Shutterstock by belizar.

As for the Fossa's snout (or mouth), it's quite short. Their ears, on the other hand, are round and big. Because of their sensitive senses, Fossas can see, hear, and smell really well. They use all their senses in hunting for prey and in avoiding predators.

Unlike cats, Fossas have a standard color. The adults have reddish brown backs with cream-colored bellies. Their coats are straight, short, and thick in appearance. They don't have patterns or spots to easily distinguish them from one another.

Young Fossas, however, have a different color – well, different from the adults, that is. As juveniles, they are either colored white or gray. However, their color will eventually change into reddish brown when they turn into adults.

Another reason to have a change in their color is when it's mating season. During this time, their belly will somewhat look orangey. The reason for this is that they have a chest gland that secretes a reddish substance during this time, turning their belly fur a different color.

Fossas live in forests where there are sources of fresh water.
Image from Shutterstock by poeticpenguin.

Where Can You Find Fossas?

Fossas can only be found in Madagascar – an island in Africa. Although there are many Fossas all over the island, the population is not that big. Madagascar is a large island, and you can find this type of animal almost everywhere.

A greater number of Fossas can be found in humid forests than in dry forests. The reason for this is that humid forests have more trees – and more trees mean there is more shade. Fossas prefer living in areas where they can rest in the shade of trees than in areas that are hot and overly exposed to the sun – such as in dry forests.

As with most wild animals, Fossas also like to live in undisturbed forests. While they are used to the presence of other animals, they certainly don't appreciate the presence of humans. Fortunately, there are protected areas in Madagascar – these have limited human activities because hunting animals is not allowed in such places.

Fossas have long tails.
Image from Shutterstock by poeticpenguin.

How Fossas Behave

Fossas are cathemeral creatures. This is different from diurnal animals that are active during the day and nocturnal creatures which are more active at night. As cathemeral animals, Fossas are active in both daytime and nighttime.

Of course, they are not awake all throughout the day and night. Unlike diurnal animals that sleep continuously at night, they are active during the late afternoon and sometimes around midnight because they are hungry, and need to hunt for food. Unlike nocturnal creatures that mostly spend the daytime sleeping, Fossas are quite active early in the morning because again, they are hunting for food. Basically their day consists of hunting, feeding, sleeping and repeating this process as necessary.

Do Fossas have homes? Well, they consider the entire forest their home. As for a particular place where they return to every day, the males don't usually do this. As they hunt and look for food, they just sleep and rest anywhere in the vicinity.

Fossas are solitary animals – they are usually alone.
Image from Shutterstock by poeticpenguin.

The males are usually solitary as well. It's very seldom that you will see male Fossas in groups, even in small groups of two to three. When this does happen, it's usually for cooperative hunting – which means that they have agreed to hunt down a prey (a big one that's hard to defeat all alone) and share the food among themselves.

For the females, it's quite different, especially when they have offspring to take care of. In this case, the mother Fossa will choose a place where she can nurse and take care of her young while they are dependent on her.

A beautiful Fossa.
Image from Shutterstock by Dudarev Mikhail.

Note that Fossas are not aggressive animals. In fact, it's very seldom that Fossas fight with one another. The only time that they can get aggressive and violent is when it's mating season and the males are competing for the attention of the females. In this case, they can really get into a fight and hurt one another. However, this situation is not unusual for most wild animals because they usually behave that way when it's mating season. After the mating season is over, everything will go back to normal and they can all live peacefully in the same forest again.

Fossas that have been observed in captivity also showed that they are wild animals that can be somewhat tamed. When they trust a human, they will allow him or her (such as a zookeeper) to touch them. The females, however, are said to be friendlier than the males. Adult males, in particular, have a tendency to bite when touched.

Fossas are wild animals.
Image from Shutterstock by belizar.

Diet

Fossas are basically carnivorous animals – which means that they mostly eat meat. In the forest, their choices of prey include lemurs (their favorite food), rodents, birds, and reptiles.

With their natural ability to chase prey on the ground and in trees, they always have an opportunity to find food easily (as long as these animals are available). There are also times when they go on group hunts and cooperate with one another. It's not unusual for two Fossas, for example, to chase after a prey in a tree until it falls – and then there will be other Fossas waiting on the ground to catch the animal.

Fossas are carnivorous animals.
Image from Shutterstock by Dmitry Shkurin

How Do Fossas Communicate?

You know how people communicate with each other, right? Humans talk with each other and use words to express themselves.

Well, animals communicate with one another too, but in a different language. In the case of Fossas, they can use their voice to communicate. Like cats, they can give off a purring sound, too (if you have a cat, you are surely familiar with the purring sound). They can also make a loud sound to frighten off an enemy or a predator. If they are scared, their voice will come out nervous and they will gasp for breath, too. Sometimes, they will even scream in a high pitched voice to attract other Fossas – they usually do this during mating season to attract females.

The females make a special sound when mating. If you are familiar with the meow of a cat, it's something similar to that. The voice, of course, is louder and deeper than that of a cat, because the Fossa is a bigger animal.

During mating season, the males also make some strange sounds. They sigh and grunt when they find a female that's ready for mating.

Fossas make strange sounds when it's mating season.
Image from Shutterstock by belizar.

The Fossa's form of communication is not limited to vocal sounds – they also use scents. Scent marking is considered to be a form of communication because it tells other animals about the presence of other creatures in the same environment or territory.

In the case of Fossas, they leave their scents on trees, rocks, and even on the ground. They have an anal gland that releases liquid substance – and they use that for scent marking. Don't forget about their chest glands too, which they particularly use during the mating season. With this gland, other Fossas are made aware that it's that time of the year for breeding.

Fossas have a good sense of balance.
Image from Shutterstock by belizar.

Breeding and Reproduction

In Madagascar, the mating season for Fossas usually happens from September to October. During this time, as many as eight males will want to mate with one female.

To get the female's attention, the male will use its voice and make different kinds of sounds. It will also behave aggressively towards other males (those that also want to mate with the female).

Fossas usually give birth to one to six offspring.
Image from Shutterstock by belizar.

The gestation period (or time of pregnancy) is about 90 days, after which, the female Fossa will give birth to a litter of young Fossas (about one to six individuals). The young ones are born blind and toothless, so they will be totally dependent on their mother for food.

At about two weeks, the young's eyes will be open, and at about three months, they can start eating solid food. It will take about a year, however, for young Fossas to be totally independent. When they reach three to four years, they will be ready for breeding and reproduction.

A Fossa climbing up a tree.
Image from Shutterstock by belizar.

Life Span of Fossa

Fossas can live for up to 20 years. Being one of the biggest animals in Madagascar, they have very few predators. During their lifetime, they breed and multiply to increase their population.

Status

Because of their small population, Fossas are vulnerable to extinction. If they all die, they will become extinct.

Note that they only give birth to a few individuals per breeding season – and the usual number of offspring is only about two to three. That's actually one of the reasons why there aren't that many.

A Fossa in captivity.
Image from Shutterstock by Sergey Didenko.

Also, destruction of forests can lead to their death because other animals will become scarce. If they don't have enough food to eat, they will starve to death. This is precisely the reason why protected areas are now enacted in Madagascar to protect their environment.

If you can't go to Madagascar to see these wonderful creatures, look for Fossas in your local zoos. A lot of zoos are now breeding Fossas to keep the species alive for a long time.

Disclaimer

The information contained in this book is for general information purposes only. The information is provided by the authors and, while we endeavor to keep the information up to date and correct, we make no representations or warranties of any kind, expressed or implied, about the completeness, accuracy, reliability, suitability or availability with respect to the book or the information, products, services, or related graphics contained in the book for any purpose. Any reliance you place on such information is therefore strictly at your own risk.

Made in the USA
Lexington, KY
01 February 2018